WATER CYCLE

Frances Purslow

www.av2books.com

BOOK CODE

W 3 1 9 1 5 0

AV² by Weigl brings you media enhanced books that support active learning.

AV² provides enriched content that supplements and complements this book. Weigl's AV² books strive to create inspired learning and engage young minds for a total learning experience.

Go to **www.av2books.com**, and enter this book's unique code. You will have access to video, audio, web links, quizzes, a slide show, and activities.

Audio
Listen to sections of the book read aloud.

Video
Watch informative video clips.

Web Link
Find research sites and play interactive games.

Try This!
Complete activities and hands-on experiments.

Due to the dynamic nature of the Internet, some of the URLs and activities provided as part of AV² by Weigl may have changed or ceased to exist. AV² by Weigl accepts no responsibility for any such changes. All media enhanced books are regularly monitored to update addresses and sites in a timely manner. Contact AV² by Weigl at 1-866-649-3445 or av2books@weigl.com with any questions, comments, or feedback.

Published by AV² by Weigl
350 5th Avenue, 59th Floor
New York, NY 10118
Website: www.av2books.com   www.weigl.com

Library of Congress Cataloging-in-Publication Data

Purslow, Frances.
 The water cycle / Frances Purslow.
   p. cm. -- (Science matters. Water science)
 Includes index.
 ISBN 978-1-61690-003-8 (hardcover : alk. paper) -- ISBN 978-1-61690-009-0 (softcover : alk. paper) -- ISBN 978-1-61690-015-1 (e-book)
 1. Hydrologic cycle--Juvenile literature. I. Title.
 GB848.P87 2011
 551.48078--dc22
                       2009050982

Printed in the United States of America in North Mankato, Minnesota
1 2 3 4 5 6 7 8 9 0 14 13 12 11 10

052010
WEP264000

Project Coordinator Heather C. Hudak
Design Terry Paulhus

Photo Credits
Every reasonable effort has been made to trace ownership and to obtain permission to reprint copyright material. The publishers would be pleased to have any errors or omissions brought to their attention so that they may be corrected in subsequent printings.

Weigl acknowledges Getty Images as its primary image supplier for this title.
World Resources Institute: Pages 12–13 map source.

CONTENTS

It is a long and difficult process to clean the water that comes out of household taps. Some activities that require water, such as watering lawns or washing cars, do not need tap water. **Recycling** water is one way to help prevent using valuable water resources for such activities. Rainwater can be collected and used to wash cars, and recycled house water can be used to water lawns.

Studying the Water Cycle

Water covers more than 70 percent of Earth's surface. It is found in oceans, rivers, ponds, and puddles. Water is also found in air. Every day, water disappears into the sky. It also returns to the ground. This process is called the water cycle. Sunshine, air, water, and the force of **gravity** work together as part of the water cycle. Over time, all streams, rivers, and lakes flow into the ocean. This is an important part of the water cycle.

Most of Earth's water is liquid. Water can also be a gas or a solid. Each one of these forms is called a phase. Every day, the Sun heats 1 trillion tons (907 billion tonnes) of water in oceans and on land. The heated water becomes water vapor.

Less than one percent of Earth's water is vapor. Water vapor may be invisible. It may also appear as fog, clouds, or steam.

Solid water is in the form of ice, snow, hail, and frost. About two percent of Earth's water is found in **icecaps**, **glaciers**, and other forms of ice and snow.

■ Only one percent of Earth's water is available for people to use. The rest is salty or frozen.

Molecule Movement and Condensation

Water is made of water **molecules**. The molecules in liquid water cling together. When water is heated, some of the molecules separate from the liquid.

Water seems to disappear because the Sun heats the water and the air around it. The water actually changes into a different form. We can no longer see it, so we say it has disappeared.

STATES OF WATER

The diagrams below show particles in the three states of water.

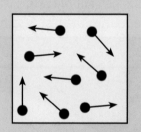

Particles of a liquid
In liquid water, particles are farther apart. They have enough energy to move around, but they are still attracted to each other. People can hold liquid water in their hands, but it will run out of their hands.

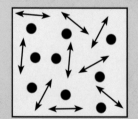

Particles of a solid
In a solid, particles are closer together. They have enough energy to vibrate, but they cannot move around. People can hold water in this state without difficulty.

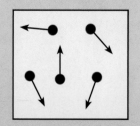

Particles of a gas
As a gas, particles have enough energy to move around and overpower attraction. They spread out much farther and are free to move in ways that a solid and liquid cannot. Water in this state can be contained only in a completely sealed area.

Condensation is the process of water vapor changing to liquid water. After a bath or shower, the bathroom mirror is often steamy. Soon, drops of water appear and trickle down the mirror. This happens because the mirror's surface is cooler than the air in the bathroom. It is the result of condensation.

Water molecules move more slowly as they cool. Sometimes, they slow enough to grab onto one another. Then, the water vapor condenses into tiny droplets.

■ Cold air outdoors can cause condensation on glass windows indoors.

Clouds and Precipitation

Water droplets form clouds when water **evaporates** and **water vapor** condenses around tiny pieces of dust. Most days, clouds cover more than half of Earth's surface. Clouds move water from oceans to dry land.

Clouds also act as a giant blanket for Earth. The blanket prevents too much sunshine from reaching Earth. Too much sunshine would evaporate all of Earth's water.

CLOUD CLASSIFICATIONS

The shape a cloud takes depends on many factors, such as temperature, pressures, and wind. Here are some cloud classifications.

Altocumulus   **Altostratus**   **Cirrus**   **Cumulonimbus**

Cumulus   **Nimbostratus**   **Stratocumulus**   **Stratus**

Over time, so much water condenses that a cloud cannot hold any more. The cloud grows heavy, and the water falls to Earth. Water that falls to Earth in solid or liquid form is called precipitation.

■ If 1 square mile (2.6 square kilometers) of land receives 1 inch (2.5 centimeters) of rainfall, a total of more than 17 million gallons (64 million liters) of water will cover the land.

Forms of Condensation and Precipitation

As water vapor in the air condenses, it takes many different forms. Here are some of the main forms water vapor takes.

CLOUDS

- Masses of water vapor that float high in the sky
- An important part of the water cycle because they allow water to travel around the globe

DEW

- Water vapor that condenses on plants after a cool night
- In low temperatures, will freeze and form as frost

FROST

- Frozen water vapor or dew that forms during condensation
- Similar to dew, but needs a sub-zero temperature to form

FOG

- A cloud that forms near the ground
- Little difference between clouds and fog

Precipitation returns water to Earth. It falls when clouds grow too heavy and cannot hold more water. Precipitation takes many forms.

HAIL

- Consists of balls of ice that form when the temperature is just below freezing

RAIN

- Water droplets that fall in temperatures above freezing
- Large raindrops fall faster than small raindrops.

SLEET

- A form of melting snow or freezing rain

SNOW

- Forms when air near the ground is at or near freezing temperatures

Access to Fresh Water Around the World

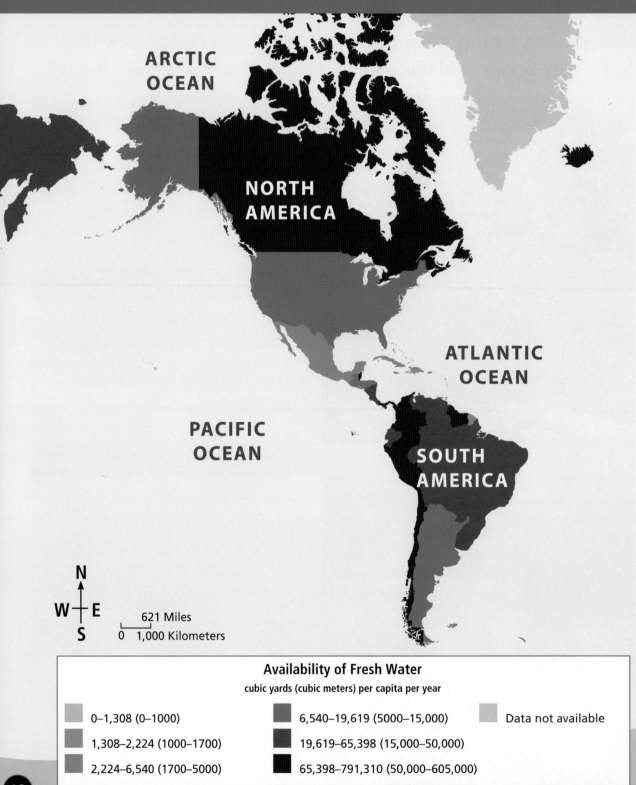

ARCTIC OCEAN

NORTH AMERICA

ATLANTIC OCEAN

PACIFIC OCEAN

SOUTH AMERICA

N W E S

621 Miles
0   1,000 Kilometers

Availability of Fresh Water
cubic yards (cubic meters) per capita per year

- 0–1,308 (0–1000)
- 1,308–2,224 (1000–1700)
- 2,224–6,540 (1700–5000)
- 6,540–19,619 (5000–15,000)
- 19,619–65,398 (15,000–50,000)
- 65,398–791,310 (50,000–605,000)
- Data not available

This map shows how much fresh water is available to countries around the world. Use this map and other sources to answer the following questions.

1. Which countries have the most fresh water?
2. Which countries have the least fresh water?

ARCTIC OCEAN

ASIA

EUROPE

AFRICA

PACIFIC OCEAN

ATLANTIC OCEAN

INDIAN OCEAN

AUSTRALIA

SOUTHERN OCEAN

ANTARCTICA

Transpiration and Evaporation

Plants help move moisture into the air. The roots of trees and other plants **absorb** water from the soil. The water flows up the plant's stem or trunk. It passes along the branches to the leaves. Inside the leaves, the plant uses some of the water to make food. Often, there is more water in the leaves than the plant needs. The extra water escapes into the air from the surface of the leaves. This process is called transpiration.

Often, after it rains, puddles remain on the road. Over time, the puddles disappear, or evaporate. Water evaporates more quickly or slowly depending on wind, temperature, and **humidity**.

■ Through transpiration, a single tree can release as much as 70 gallons (265 liters) of water into the atmosphere each day.

Water Cycle Timeline

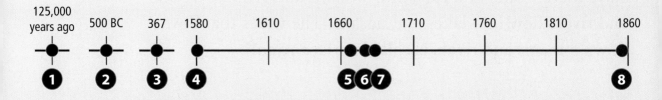

125,000 years ago — 500 BC — 367 — 1580 — 1610 — 1660 — 1710 — 1760 — 1810 — 1860

1 **2** **3** **4** **5 6 7** **8**

1 **About 125,000 years ago**
Oceans are about 18 feet (5.5 meters) higher than they are today.

2 **500 BC**
Ancient civilizations understand the water cycle process.

3 **About 367**
Aristotle makes observations regarding the water cycle process.

4 **1580 AD**
Bernard Palissy develops the theory of the water cycle. Several years later, the theory is confirmed by Pierre Perrault.

5 **1674**
De l'origine des fontaines, or "On the origin of springs," by Pierre Perrault, is published.

6 **1686**
Physicist Edme Mariotte confirms Perrault's research.

7 **1687**
Edmond Halley proves that the amount of evaporation from the ocean and rain is enough to keep rivers filled.

8 **1859**
John Tyndall finds that certain gases, such as water vapor, trap heat and help keep Earth's surface air temperature within a comfortable range.

Melting and Runoff

Some of the rain that falls to Earth soaks into the ground and stays there. Some rain runs into streams and rivers. Streams and rivers flow into lakes and oceans. The water that flows down streams and rivers is called surface **runoff**.

Water from melted snow, sleet, and hail also flows into rivers and streams or soaks into the ground. Over time, this water returns to the air and falls again as precipitation. The type and amount of precipitation, as well as how long the precipitation lasts, affects the amount of runoff.

Much of the precipitation that falls to Earth is carried underground by runoff. Underground water is called groundwater. Groundwater is found in soil and in the cracks and spaces between rocks and sand.

Due to runoff, any chemicals or waste from land will most likely end up a part of the water cycle. Runoff carries **pollutants** from the land to bodies of water and **reservoirs** used for drinking and cleaning. This is harmful to the environment and its inhabitants. The majority of toxins and chemicals found in water supplies originates from land sources, such as car washes and farms. By preventing land pollution, one can keep water supplies fresh and clean.

Groundwater moves slowly through layers of earth, nourishing plants along the way. It later joins major bodies of water such as rivers, lakes, and oceans. Groundwater can be found almost everywhere. It is refilled by runoff.

THE WATER CYCLE

1 Water in Oceans, Lakes, and Rivers
Oceans, lakes, and rivers are bodies of water where large amounts of water sit or travel to even larger bodies of water.

2 Evaporation
The Sun heats water in bodies of water. This turns the water into a gas so that it will rise into the air.

3 Condensation
Once it rises to a certain height, water in the form of gas cools and condenses into clouds.

4 Water Storage in the Atmosphere
Clouds can stay in the air for a period of time. Then, clouds are moved around by wind currents. Clouds collide and become larger.

5 Precipitation
When clouds become too big, water begins to fall from them. The water falls to land as precipitation.

6 Surface Runoff
Once on land, water flows into oceans, lakes, and rivers. There, it will begin the cycle again.

Pollution

People need to take care of water because it recycles forever. Air and water pollution can harm water and the water cycle.

Some factories and vehicles add chemicals to the air. Chemicals poured on the ground or floating in the sky enter the water. Water molecules in the air cling to the pollutants and form clouds. The pollutants mix with water and fall to Earth as rain or snow. These chemicals can destroy crops, trees, and lakes. They can also hurt animals and people. Once the chemicals are in the water, it is difficult to remove them.

Scientists believe pollution particles in the air may affect the water cycle. The more pollution there is in an area, the more particles are in the air. Water droplets form around pollution particles, resulting in smaller droplets.

What is a Hydrologist?

A hydrologist is someone who studies water. Some hydrologists research ways to solve problems relating to water, such as pollution, erosion, or lack of availability.

Luke Howard

Luke Howard studied nature and was interested in many kinds of science. In 1802, he sorted clouds into four groups based on their appearance. He used Latin words to describe the clouds in each group.

The four basic kinds of clouds are stratus, cumulus, cirrus, and nimbus. Layered clouds, low to the ground are called stratus. Cumulus clouds are large, white, and fluffy. High, wispy clouds are called cirrus. Nimbus is the term for dark rain clouds.

Working Conditions
Hydrologists do research in offices as well as outdoors. The days can be quite long, and, sometimes, hydrologists must be away from home for weeks while doing research in remote places.

Tools
Hydrologists use many tools, including shovels and computers, for different kinds of research.

Eight Facts About the Water Cycle

Earth's water has always been part of the water cycle. There is about the same amount of water on Earth now as there was when Earth was formed billions of years ago.

Less than 1000th of one percent of Earth's water is contained in the bodies of living creatures.

More than 97 percent of Earth's water is located in the oceans. Ocean water is salt water.

More than 90 percent of the world's fresh water is contained in the ice covering Antarctica.

Ocean water is salty. Salt does not evaporate, so rain water is fresh.

Only about 0.005 percent of Earth's water moves through the water cycle at any time.

Hurricanes need warm, moist ocean air to form, stay strong, and grow. If a hurricane travels over land, away from the ocean, it loses its power.

In 20 minutes, one thunderstorm can produce more than 125,000,000 gallons (473,176,473 L) of water.

Water Cycle
Brain Teasers

1 How much of Earth is covered with water?

2 Who named the types of clouds?

3 What is water called when it is a gas?

4 What is the name for large, white, fluffy clouds?

5 What is a cloud of water vapor near the ground called?

6 How do clouds protect Earth?

7 Name four types of solid water.

8 How much of Earth's water is located in oceans?

9 Name four types of precipitation.

10 When a puddle dries up, where does the water go?

ANSWERS: 1. More than 70 percent 2. Luke Howard 3. Water vapor 4. Cumulus 5. Fog 6. Clouds act as a blanket, protecting Earth from receiving too much sunshine. 7. Snow, ice, frost, and hail 8. More than 97 percent 9. Rain, snow, sleet, and hail 10. It evaporates into the air.

Science in Action

Testing Transpiration

Plant leaves add water vapor to the air. The needles of evergreen trees also add water vapor to the air. Find out whether plants with needles produce the same amount of water as plants with leaves.

2 clear plastic bags

a fresh plant stem with a leaf on it

a fresh plant stem with needles on it

2 glasses of water

2 elastic bands

Directions

1 Place a plastic bag over each stem. Fasten the bag tightly around each stem using an elastic band.

2 Fill each glass halfway with water.

3 Place one stem in each glass, and place the glasses in a sunny place.

4 In 30 minutes, check the bags. Which bag has more water in it? Do needles or leaves give off more water?

Words to Know

absorb: soak up

evaporates: disappears into the air; the process of liquid water changing to water vapor

glaciers: large masses of ice in cold regions

gravity: the force that pulls objects toward the center of Earth

humidity: water vapor in the air, or dampness

icecaps: sheets of ice that cover an area of land

molecules: the smallest pieces that a substance can be divided into without changing it into another substance

pollutants: harmful materials such as gases, chemicals, and waste that dirty air, water, and soil

recycling: returning to an original condition so a process can begin again

reservoirs: large natural or humanmade lakes that are used as a water source

runoff: water not absorbed by soil

water vapor: water in gas form

Index

Log on to www.av2books.com

AV[2] by Weigl brings you media enhanced books that support active learning. Go to **www.av2books.com**, and enter the special code inside the front cover of this book. You will gain access to enriched and enhanced content that supplements and complements this book. Content includes video, audio, web links, quizzes, a slide show, and activities.

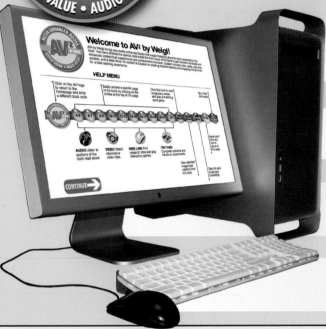

Audio
Listen to sections of the book read aloud.

Video
Watch informative video clips.

Web Link
Find research sites and play interactive games.

Try This!
Complete activities and hands-on experiments.

WHAT'S ONLINE?

Try This! Complete activities and hands-on experiments.	**Web Link** Find research sites and play interactive games.	**Video** Watch informative video clips.	**EXTRA FEATURES**
Pages 6-7 Try this activity about the states of water	**Pages 8-9** Find out more about cloud classifications	**Pages 4-5** Watch a video about the water cycle	**Audio** Hear introductory audio at the top of every page
Pages 12-13 See if you can identify parts of the world that have the most and the least access to fresh water	**Pages 16-17** Link to more information about groundwater	**Pages 10-11** Check out a video about types of condensation and precipitation	**Key Words** Study vocabulary, and play a matching word game.
Pages 14-15 Use this timeline activity to test your knowledge of world events	**Pages 18-19** Learn more about being a hydrologist	**Pages 14-15** Watch a video about transpiration and evaporation	**Slide Show** View images and captions, and try a writing activity.
Pages 18-19 Write about a day in the life of a hydrologist	**Page 20** Link to facts about the water cycle		**AV[2] Quiz** Take this quiz to test your knowledge
Page 22 Try the activity in the book, then play an interactive game			